BLOOD MOON

Also by Patricia Kirkpatrick

Odessa
Century's Road

BLOOD MOON

Poems

Patricia Kirkpatrick

MILKWEED EDITIONS

Published 2020 by Milkweed Editions

Printed in the United States of America

Cover design by Mary Austin Speaker

Cover art: *Woman Reaching*, 1980, Glass and wire, 10 x 6 x 6 inches by Joey Kirkpatrick
        and Flora C. Mace

20 21 22 23 24   5 4 3 2 1

First Edition

Milkweed Editions, an independent nonprofit publisher, gratefully acknowledges sustaining support from the Alan B. Slifka Foundation and its president, Riva Ariella Ritvo-Slifka; the Ballard Spahr Foundation; *Copper Nickel*; the Jerome Foundation; the McKnight Foundation; the National Endowment for the Arts; the National Poetry Series; the Target Foundation; and other generous contributions from foundations, corporations, and individuals. Also, this activity is made possible by the voters of Minnesota through a Minnesota State Arts Board Operating Support grant, thanks to a legislative appropriation from the arts and cultural heritage fund. For a full listing of Milkweed Editions supporters, please visit milkweed.org.

Names: Kirkpatrick, Patricia, author.

Title: Blood moon : poems / Patricia Kirkpatrick.

Description: First Edition. | Minneapolis, Minnesota : Milkweed Editions, 2020. | Summary: "Blood Moon is a collection of poems examining racism, whiteness, and language within one woman's life"—Provided by publisher.

Identifiers: LCCN 2019041221 (print) | LCCN 2019041222 (ebook) | ISBN 9781571314987 (trade paperback) | ISBN 9781571319739 (ebook)

Subjects: LCGFT: Poetry.

Classification: LCC PS3561.I7135 B56 2020 (print) | LCC PS3561.I7135 (ebook) | DDC 811/.54--dc23

LC record available at https://lccn.loc.gov/2019041221

LC ebook record available at https://lccn.loc.gov/2019041222

Milkweed Editions is committed to ecological stewardship. We strive to align our book production practices with this principle, and to reduce the impact of our operations in the environment. We are a member of the Green Press Initiative, a nonprofit coalition of publishers, manufacturers, and authors working to protect the world's endangered forests and conserve natural resources. *Blood Moon* was printed on acid-free 30% postconsumer-waste paper by Versa Press.

For my sisters, Kristine Kirkpatrick, Joey Kirkpatrick,
and Tracy Kirkpatrick, and Flora Mace

CONTENTS

. . . that the moon was witness to the event and that the event was
witness to the moon . . . that even a cup of tea is subject to lunar tides
—MARY RUEFLE

No world is lost in the stories.
Everything is lost in the retelling,
in being wondered at. We grow up
and grow old in our land of grass
and blood moons, birth and goneness.

—LINDA GREGG

A traveler, not understanding the bird's motive,
notes the beauty of its ruffled, fog-colored hood
as it rises.

—KATHLEEN FRASER

BLOOD MOON

I

TRAVELER

The moon skips its stone across the river,
lulling the city sky before dusk.

What price do you pay for safety?
What clue tells you to run?

Going home, tired commuters
pray over cellphones, doze
above newspapers, exhausted
by stories of trysts
and portents of oil and guns.

Where do you believe harm comes from?

Wake up you lazy ones
a child scolds fellow passengers
in a language she's losing
as she travels between two mothers.

On the train of muddy shoes and apple cores,
she falls asleep, dreaming of change
and coral geraniums.

The moon spreads its light like circles
a stone casts, the sound
across water
like a cello being bowed.

What, when it's started, has to keep going?
Will there be someone to meet you?

RECESS

At recess we sang over ropes
turning in circles
and when we were ready,
jumped in.
Read. Remember. Repeat.
A robin isn't really
red. Rabbit. River. Wren.
The rule of the lemon is juice
if you roll it. M-I-S-S-
I-S-S-I-
P-P-I. The river's expected
to crest. All night
fathers fill sandbags.
You can turn if you don't want to jump.
To live near the flood runs a risk.
One rabbit reveals the hawk.
You're out if your foot gets caught
or you cross the rickety bridge.

MARBLES, 1957

Squatting in crop grass,
we hit cat eyes with steelies

until called in from recess
to read and write in the classroom.

Letters made words
we learned
outside and in school,
at home, on television.
Polio. Segregate.
Little Rock. Vaccinate.

To decide who shoots first
we changed one word
when we played. *Eenie meenie*
miney mo. Catch a ...

Tiger. We said *tiger.*

Some words you don't say
but you know. *Holler, holler.*

Let them go.

LEARNING TO READ, 1963

Begin with *A*.
Apple. *Black*. The letters line up
like train cars. Start then stop.
You won't lose your place.

Cane. Continue. *Can*.
Long *a* says its name; short
prefers not to be forced.
Some letters stay silent:
to knead is to press or to blend.

But the chaperone said
Negro girls wouldn't be happy
if we let them join us.
We didn't say anything.
Just waited, tickets in hand,
until we heard the conductor call
All aboard
and rode away.

THE FLOWER THAT DOESN'T COME BACK

We were bored and couldn't go swimming.
Polio fizzed like wasps in the pools.

Down the street a deaf girl with red hair
twirled and twirled in her yard
unfurling
the silence I imagined inside her.

Mothers pinned laundry all morning
to lines between days.

On a tree bark, a locust
left the whole shape of a life.
Transparent. Brittle.

Afternoon showed war and cartoons
saving the real war and its blizzards
of gas for later.

At night when the programs stopped
the screen gagged on static and numbers.

Marigolds, zinnias, snapdragons
where we galloped dolls and plastic horses
never let on.

Summer ended.
At school I felt small yet magic.
Beginning was always the same.
Go back to the sky and start over.

Readers gave directions.
Look, look. Run, run.

If you were going to get out, you would have to give up
believing there wouldn't be harm.

ARRIVING IN BALTIMORE

Where the city begins, there's water
and a barren harbor,
blocks of glass shopping malls
tourists forage.
Once in pens here, adjacent to wharves,
traders kept Africans, captured
and shackled
before being *sold south*.
My cab keeps going, past
muddy lots, chain link,
men lugging plastic sacks of belongings.
Delivered to a modest hotel,
I get pleasantries at the front desk.
Maids push carts down the hall.
I unpack in a room without a Gideon
in the musty drawer.
Why would I expect to feel blameless?

BALTIMORE, 2015:
fragments after the death of Freddie Gray

after Adrienne Rich

Some days students throw pencils at each other.
Some days they study fractions,

look for a common denominator.

Half an apple, cups of carrots, three pieces
of pizza, a pint of milk in the lunchroom.

Some days need a subject and an action
or a state of being because it's grammar.

The cop shot. The man was dead.

The city declares a sky of emergency
with a rave of chopper blades.

Mourners light rage like rockets.
Schools close. Stores shatter. Streets of glass,

whole cordons throb—
Tell it to the forest fire; tell it to the moon. . .

Some days there is nothing to eat.

When you make places bad
you're making it hard for
people to get food.

FEAR RATTLES A SILVER BELL

A dream, when it's over, doesn't close
like a shop door,

its silver bell rattling,

but steeps like loose tea leaves.
Grievance is cut with slices of lemon,
the dull knife askew on the counter.

And when you wake up, pretend
your new neighbor finished
mowing his lawn last night. Nobody noticed
his skin color.
Nobody called the police.

Pretend it was only a dream.

The police didn't come. The police
didn't knock on his door
and ask if he lived in the house.
Nobody asked him to prove it.

THE MOON, A CENTO, A CLOAK OF PATCHES

There are words and there are deeds, and both

are dying out, dying away
from where they were and what they meant.
—MAURICE MANNING

The little river lying on its back in the sun or the sun or
The varying moon changing over the changing hills
Constant.

. . . Was the moon a good
sign? Should we trust how it silvers
the hills and follow after it?

The moon plays horn, leaning on the shoulder of the dark universe
to the infinite glitter of chance.

It is almost not there,
Like a watch with a black face
You dropped down the well of your childhood.

. . . like a lost language that has no word for harm

The Moon was but a Chin of Gold
A Night or two ago —
And now she turns Her perfect Face
Upon the World below —

. . . a coin of moonlight on the shattered place

Coming to strange countries refugee children find
land burned over by winter.

Ruined hills and towns without roofs on the houses.
Men and women in black clothing offering water.

Wide under this moon they stand gathering fire.

The message arrives, but there is no one to sign for it.

What then of the moon,
the room, the bed, the poetry . . . ?

Who will be watching then, who
listening? How will the things that are
coming be noticed by those who never
look up? The moon will be there.

WHAT WAS COMING

We didn't see what was coming.
Bridges collapsed
and schools didn't have enough chairs.

There was meat made with paper for dinner.
Disarray and foreclosure in houses.
Workers stood for hours at fluorescent stations,
came home with fists
clutching water.

When I heard shouting, I put on my shoes and ran.

Women carried mace for protection.
Children hid in concrete walls from gunshots.
Field corn was poisoned. Birds
tore scapular wings on burnt sky.
Who betrayed us?
Why has the well gone dry?

PATRIARCH

Because she married without his permission,
the father stoned his daughter to death.

NEW ROOF

The men came at dawn with hammers
and began to work in the dark,

unfastening shingles from pallets,
angling ladders,
climbing overhead with cleats
and ropes attached to their belts.

All day, as the heat rose, men tore, flung,
and hammered, charring
the yard with heaves of old shingles,
searing the pitch of the house
with the *pock, pock* of nail guns.

When you order a roof, you're asked to choose
a color for the shingles, and if you want
Mexican workers or American.

The guarantee comes with the contract.
No storm will leak or force entry now.

THE BORDER

The world will soon break up into small colonies of the saved.

—ROBERT BLY, "THOSE BEING EATEN BY AMERICA"

They begin taking children from their parents.
We already know the story it's like.

You know the one. When there isn't enough
food or safety, at night
a brother and sister, seized, get sent
to the woods. A swamp, the desert . . .

They might have stones
or crumbs in their pockets.
Sometimes they get bread. Sometimes
milk or berries.

The border marks a line
the way a strike of lightning
leaves one house standing
burns down the next.

For some children there's nothing
but ashes and scraps.
That's how much the border matters ·

when you reach the makeshift tables,
when you're questioned in a language
you don't understand,

when a witch squeezing a bony finger
figures out how to profit.

Terror begins a jangle of keys and belts.
The children go in cages.

LION

for Melinda Ward

When the lion came through the camp,
one woman sat up in her tent, breathing
the terrible smell.

Next morning the guide said *no*
when she asked then *yes but
don't tell the others.*

Sleep in a tent, dream with creatures . . .
The night breathes and stirs.

If you wait before using a lamp,
your eyes will adjust
and you can see farther in the dark.

How do you know? How do you
ever know?

II

THE SCHOOL BUS

In late afternoon, yellow buses
line up at the curb, waiting
to take children home.
They've been in school for hours,
following rules, learning
the names and shapes of countries,
feeding small animals in cages.
Now they carry long division
up the steps
to a ride stuffed with mittens and fists,
words for body parts,
and the colors of each other's skin.
Some children, of course, are buoyant,
knocking into each other
like puppies in a cardboard box.
Others slump quietly against
smeared windows,
exhausted by what they know.

LESSONS

At the library you check out your quota.
Stories with royalty
or herds of wild horses.

Mustang, crown, line of succession.
Quarrel means *fight* the way *grip*
means *suitcase*.
German measles mean *quarantine*.

Corn, maize, Indian, native—
Cassius Clay changed his name to Muhammad Ali.
Refused to go in the army.

Quicksand goes with *canyon*
in the movies. *Monarch* with *milkweed*.
Radio, cicada, a cage
lined with newspaper—*quotidian*
means the real world.

The daughter's sent into the forest, the ballerina
takes a deep bow.

Nine planets have names
and quiver. At night, the moon
spreads the bed with white pages.
Fighter. Dancer. Queen.

GHOSTS

St. Joseph Church and Elementary School, San Francisco, 1983

The nuns still wore white habits
and put a finger to their lips
when the priest came into a classroom.

The children had old-fashioned names,
Armond, Violaine, Custodio,
and repeated the precisions of mass

wearing bottle-blue uniforms,
still crazy about *Star Wars* and SweetTarts
at recess. They had stopped saying

their families ate dogs but in summer
went back to the islands
to see *tiyas*, sleep in houses on stilts,

eat without recrimination.
When I was going at the Philippines
Redino wrote in Sister Corazon's class

I saw a fish that was drawn by clouds.
The moon often came to their poems,
birds with wings of perspiration,

hay roofs in Bicol, mangoes,
martial law. Uncles, their names cherished
or forbidden, disappeared in the night.

After the damage of Loma Prieta, nuns
returned to Manila. Lay teachers, families
couldn't afford city rent. An entrepreneur

bought the abandoned church, converted
the sanctuary to galleries and offices,
part art society, part Silicon Valley.

Ghosts run away when they open the lights.

SONG ON THE ISLAND

These boats are coming from a far place. . .

Birds fly into fringed trees.

Sometimes the days are as hot as fire
burning in another fire.

Sometimes the windows are a little bit broken.

Night opens nets in the dark.

You try to speak out of your star and sky.

Sometimes you have to go into someone very deep
to write their song.
The song teaches you to be the person you are.

The moon breaks notes across water.

I will be the hawk
and you, the frail flower
broken by the linguistic wind.

A SORT OF FAIR WONDER AND STILLNESS

There seems nothing of the modern world here—no houses,
no contrivances, only a sort of fair wonder and stillness, an
openness which has not been violated.

    —D. H. LAWRENCE, *ETRUSCAN PLACES*

I woke remembering the girl,
facing us
as she sat cross-legged in the path,
a parrot in the palmetto beside her.

We had to walk around her
to reach the ruins. She looked up
but didn't speak and that was
the crossing between us.

Inside the Temple of Inscriptions,
the passages, ascending, were narrow.
Too weak to climb, I sat outside,
waiting for the others to finish, reading
a guidebook, learning the ancients
left a roof open to see the stars,

shafts of unfettered light between worlds.

HOUSE

there was a house in the forest
the moon lit a way to the door
light overlooked the threshold

clusters of animals came
ruffian, lame, or tatted
some had escaped from stanchions
others were already wild

practiced ways were abandoned
exchanged where hyssop where
thatch overcame aspiration

like a single mistake on paper
crossed out instead of erased still
shows the first mark made

THE HARD PART

You got up with the stars
so the sheep could feed before the sun
made buds on the sagebrush

too hot. That changed
the taste and the sheep
wouldn't eat.

In a year we walked thousands of miles.
But that wasn't the hard part.

Late afternoon with the earth burning up
you'd look forward to cooling but
also be dreading the dark.

You would almost die from loneliness,
just to hear a human voice.

Then a funny thing happened. In your mind
you turned a corner

and you wouldn't walk over the hill
to see someone
even if someone was there.

THE GRASSES

At the end of summer,
we took our mother's ashes in our hands,
walked into a field,
thrust fists
over bluestem and switchgrass.

The finer dust disappeared quickly,
but the larger pieces, shiny,
flared and burst before falling
into timothy, asters,
needle-and-thread.

The field was one blade
beside another,
each blade repeated, repeating
a profusion of hues,
summoned. Yielding.

We walked into the wind.
Overhead a hawk searched the field,
lingering. . .
Pinkish and gray-green,
tawny and seed-set,
the grasses kept blowing.
We left with dust lining our palms.

COYOTE

Dawn holding rain at the screen door some charcoal

sky thundered feet in black grass hiding moon the newspaper

hadn't come yet no world waited on steps to be read but

animals tracked the city a wilding again I'd been sleeping

alone for some time fiercely the juniper flashed

like a seizure ruptured then slack neighbors said they'd seen

one before I could name the rash fur ran past starless

the flank I can't say wasn't really a fox the more I kept

looking the less certain I was I remembered the tail

of what vanished such keening came when I saw

TETRAD

Blood Moon

for Nor Hall

The moon held an aura
before turning red,
silence like a tremor
just before the baby emerges.

The other side of the moon stays hidden.

Call the baby they'd said
when the baby didn't come.
Sometimes that helps.

In labor the current ran all the way
through her. To deliver the child,
its cup being poured.

Ancient. Witnessed. Said to bring gifts.

Is the baby all right? the mother is asking.
Yes a nurse answers. *She's perfect.*

New Moon, Make Believe

If you're the child,
your mother might die any minute.
If you sleep, even dreaming,
you need to be kissed.

A veil is the part of the costume you want most.
To be promised, desired,
yet hidden.

At night, wolves hack the sky into pieces.
Shoeless, you wander,
with no destination,

a single note of song that hasn't been sung.

Your friends want to quit.
You beg to keep going.

No one in the real world hears you.

BLUE MOON

When the moon is blue, it's repeated.
Full a second time.
Stout little cabins at the water's edge
are rented. Returned to.
At night, if a boat takes on water
you can radio back. There's enough light
for someone to bring you a paddle.
Even the second time.

Each hour the moon is an apple
cleaved to move across sky.
Inside the screen door, mistakes
are forgiven. You're sort of asleep
and awake at the same time,
full of the chance to start over.

WANING CRESCENT

The way light bores the dry roses
and petals of tulips fell
wild blue after mauve

as we talked of the lost

farm, field stone, the word
harrow meaning to *break up*
and *smooth over*, distinct

from the plow and planting
whole languages too disappearing

the way our mother at the end
called for the little black dog
of her grandmother's hill, asked

where are all those horses coming from?
and put out her hand

THEN CAME A DEPARTURE

That noise in the street—
it's a truck moving backward.
I know what things are.

The street confuses me.
I lose the address.
What I buy at the store.

This is how they tell me
I am not fine.
Someone must drive me home.
I'm locked in my house.

In the morning a woman comes.
I comb and toast.
I don't have names.
Words are not with me.

CONFESSION

Rinsing plates at the kitchen window,
letting hot water run over my hands.
Wasting it.

Outside a cloud blurs the moon.
The tall pine staggers,
repeating itself in the wind.

I wipe familiar cups, hand-me-down bone,
everyday porcelain.

The moon hears a full confession.

The cloud moves on, parrot tulips droop
over the table where we left
glasses, forks, the upturned tines
of expectation.

The grown children go home
after dinner. There is nothing to do
for this loneliness.

SMALL HUT OF FLOWERS

What tiny veils
the violets
weep behind.

The tulip keeps
changing, bulb, stem,
broken wing.

Oh, break my heart
but leave me
the Dutchman's breeches.

UNREQUITED

For a time the moon disappears
and a letter he says will come by mail
doesn't come.

At the café I take a small table.
The barista is pointing out pastries—
apricot, buttercream, plum—
and kinds of tea,

green that's fired quickly, black
allowed to wither.
Pu'er must be brewed without bitterness.

Keep talking I told myself
for weeks after surgery.

Keep walking backward
while you put this deck of cards in order
the therapist told me.
Not so bad she said to her colleague.
Not so much drop foot.

Diamond, heart—desire
begins with a name.
Gabardine, susurrus—the wool
of his suit
touching my face.

Stay I said.

The moon tonight will be
thin and pale, a tisane

with nothing but herbs
and dried flowers
that steeps while I wait.

NEXT MORNING

The sky is the color of milk
left outside in a saucer
all night
but the wild one, glimpsed briefly,
never came back.

IN THE NICU

for Joe and Simone

Before you can enter,
you must wash, place your arms
in the swooshing machine,

be swaddled in water
as each baby begins

before a vessel in the way of delivery,
a rupture or position
all lightning and blood

tore a wet fledgling
of flickering lungs

a mother and father can't hold
or take from the clutch
of Looney Tunes blankets,

attached to a mask,
alarm bell, breathing tube,

a tiny syringe bringing streams
of breast milk, measured
like packets of manna

anonymous women give
every newborn, cross-nursed,
as brother or sister

in milk, delivered, yours,
the others, bruised,
translucent,

fierce, mewing, meaning
to live

BABY DAYS

The baby came early and was small.
After weeks attached to tubes
for oxygen, body heat, milk,
strips of blue cloth over his eyes,
he's fine.
His mother's fine too.

I remembered his mother cried nights,
black rain in wind, her first year.
Someday you can go back
I said, gathering her in blankets,
not exactly sure what I meant.
We walked up and down the hall.

I don't know what makes a baby live
nor what we leave when we come.

Today the baby wakes in his crib
delighted to be found, lifted,
carried to the rest of the house.

After a bottle he stands in my lap,
staring out the window
as if looking back to shore
where someone is standing.

OBOE NOTES

Across the street, while I'm writing,
my neighbor practices oboe.

High wood the French call it,
the black tube with a flared bell
she blows through,
testing reeds she shaves from cane.

She plays fast, as if flipping
through pages
to find what she wants.

Through two open windows,
scales come to me.
I hear breath directed to tone as if
bellwether, lambing squall, stone
plunged down alpine slopes.

At first you don't really know
where you're going
but keep moving ahead.
Then the wagon so carefully packed
can't make the pass.

You debate what to toss,
what to keep, whether to wait
or keep climbing.

All morning I hear her secure
which notes to take over the mountain.

THE PHOTOGRAPH OF EMILY DICKINSON

After a year at the Female Seminary—
astronomy, botany, Latin—
she came home, pressed herbaria,
never stopped watching the sky

or hearing the train lap miles
by the shanties, its whistle shriek
three times to mean *turn*,
four times to blast nerve above danger.

Futile — the winds — to a Heart in port

Often friends invited her. Often
she declined,
preferring the garden and hives
slurred with bees,

her desk, letters, *dear fancy*,
looking ahead
as she does at sixteen in the dress
of the daguerreotype,
already done
with the compass and chart.

POEM WITHOUT A SUBJECT

Often I am standing on the bank of a river.
The water is low.
There is no moon to speak of.

I call it the river of clear afternoon.
The grass is shirred with violets.

The lines of the poem are so plain
you could pour water through them.

I know she'll come to the door,
knock lightly, then whisper
It's time.

NOTES

"The Moon, a Cento, a Cloak of Patches" is a cento. Each "stanza," in order, contains lines by the following: Thomas McGrath, Joyce Sutphen, Joy Harjo, Frank Stanford, Laurie Sheck, Emily Dickinson, Carolyn Forché, Muriel Rukeyser, Linda Gregg, Muriel Rukeyser, Thomas McGrath, Lucille Clifton, and Joyce Sutphen.

The line "*Tell it to the forest fire; tell it to the moon*" is from John Berryman's "Dream Song 44." The title "*Then Came a Departure*" is from Berryman's "Dream Song 1."

"The Hard Part" is adapted from an account in *Nevada: A Bicentennial History*.

ACKNOWLEDGMENTS

Grateful acknowledgment is given to editors of the following journals, in which some of these poems, sometimes in slightly different versions, first appeared: *Poetry City*, *Saint Paul Almanac*, and *Sleet*.

"Tetrad Blood Moon" was set to music by American composer Libby Larsen as part of her song cycle *The Birth Project*.

"Traveler" was read at the 2018 concerts "Christmas with Cantus: Lessons and Carols for Our Time."

I want to give deep appreciation to Carol Bly, Joan Swearingen Bosque, Peter Campion, Tim Danz, Laura David, Sally Dixon, Kathleen Fraser, Debra Frasier, Kathryn Greenback, Jenna Gruen, Jocelyn Hale, Nor Hall, Joey Kirkpatrick, Kristine Kirkpatrick, Tracy Kirkpatrick, Jim and Tana Kirkpatrick, Virginia Jenni Kirkpatrick, Eleanor Lerman, Kyra Levine, Michael Levine, Flora Mace, Margaret Todd Maitland, Jim Moore, Julie Neraas, Laura Nortwen, Naomi Shihab Nye, Dr. Janine Pingel, Chuck Sawyer, Katharine Klein Sawyer, David and Geri Schneider, John Schulz, Dr. Paul Sperduto, Joyce Sutphen, Melinda Ward, Connie Waneck, Mary Weiland, Ann Welch, Allison Wigen, and Sally Wingert. I especially thank Frances Phillips for insightful reading of these poems. Thank you to everyone at Milkweed Editions, especially Joey McGarvey, Lee Oglesby, and Mary Austin Speaker for putting books that matter into many hands and for the support and attention you've given me and my work. A great thanks goes to Chris Everett and Bill Underwood and the Everwood Farm Foundation for the vision for art and artists, a glorious residency, and the house of three sisters where some of these poems were written. I thank the vocal ensemble of Cantus, artists with whom I've been privileged to work.

I am grateful to my family, Simone Schneider, Joe Reisdorf, and Baby Griffin and Anton Schneider and Sophie Fitzsimmons-Peters, for the joy, courage, kindness, laughter, and care you give the world.

Katharine Klein Sawyer

PATRICIA KIRKPATRICK is the author of *Odessa*, awarded the first Lindquist & Vennum Prize for Poetry and the 2013 Minnesota Book Award. She also has published *Century's Road*, poetry chapbooks, and picture books. Her poems have appeared in such journals as *Prairie Schooner*, *Poetry*, and the *Threepenny Review*, and in many anthologies. Her awards include fellowships from the National Endowment for the Arts, the Bush Foundation, the Jerome Foundation, the McKnight Foundation, the Loft Literary Center, and the Minnesota State Arts Board. She has taught writing at many colleges, most recently in the University of Minnesota MFA program. She lives in Saint Paul.

milkweed
editions

Founded as a nonprofit organization in 1980,
Milkweed Editions is an independent publisher. Our mission
is to identify, nurture and publish transformative literature,
and build an engaged community around it.

milkweed.org

Interior design & typesetting by Mary Austin Speaker
Typeset in Fournier

Fournier is a typeface created by the Monotype Corporation in 1924,
based on types cut in the mid-eighteenth century by Pierre-Simon
Fournier, a French typographer. The specific cuts used as a reference
for Fournier are referred to as "St Augustin Ordinaire" in Fournier's
influential *Manuel Typographique*, published in 1764 in Paris.